A CHRISTIAN SURVIVAL MANUAL

How to Prepare for When All Hell Breaks Loose

Stephen Kurtzahn

ISBN-13: 978-1532762895
ISBN-10: 1532762895

Table of Contents

Introduction

Are you ready?

Are you ready to feed, shelter and protect yourself, your family and your loved ones if there is a major terrorist attack in our country and there is no electricity for weeks or months?

Are you ready if a major hurricane like Katrina (2005) strikes and you're unable to evacuate?

Are you ready to leave your home at a moment's notice if a nearby nuclear power plant springs a leak and radioactive gas is released and headed your way?

Are you ready if hungry looters rush down your street, searching for food to eat, things to steal and people to kill?

Are you ready if basic government services stop functioning, and there's no police or fire protection and no ambulance service?

These aren't crazy questions. I'll tell you why—

At the time I'm writing this, economists have been forecasting that we have a major recession just over the horizon, far worse than what we experienced in 2009. What will people do if government services are unable to provide for the basic needs of our unemployed and folks have to scrounge for basic necessities?

Many of us still remember the terrorist attacks of September 11, 2001. The Islamic State (ISIS) and other radical Islamic terrorist groups are threatening far worse attacks. Attacks have been occurring all over the world. Who's to say worse attacks will not occur in our own country?

Because of global warming (yes, I believe it's happening—just look at satellite photos of the polar ice cap now compared to years ago), we'll be witnessing more and larger hurricanes, tornadoes, Tsunamis and other natural disasters. Hurricane Katrina will look like child's play!

In the United States, there has been a great deal of political unrest. What if violent protests—such as what happened during the Chicago Democratic Convention of 1968—erupt in every major city of our country at one time? What if martial law is declared? What if political protests became so violent that the police and even the National Guard are unable to stem the aggression?

Rogue nations and their leaders have threatened to attack the United States with a nuclear warhead at the end of their ballistic missiles. What if these enemies of the West actually succeed in detonating a nuclear bomb far up in the atmosphere, so that all our electrical and electronic capabilities are totally fried? Are you ready to survive using the technology of 150 years ago?

We don't know what's in store for us, but it's important to be prepared. This little book is intended to give you some common sense advice and direction when it comes to disaster preparation. This book doesn't pretend to be the last word on preparing for natural or man-made disasters. I'm not a "prepper," nor do I want to be considered one. I'm not a white supremacist nor do I belong to a militia. But I do believe that you can prepare for potential breakdowns in society by using items you already have in your home or by purchasing items a little at a time as you go about your regular daily shopping.

As a believer in Jesus Christ, I also want to share with you what God's Word, the Bible, has to say about preparing for unknown problems or disasters. I'm not a Mormon and I'm not a millennialist, either. I'm not waiting for a rapture, or seven years of tribulation or even a millennial kingdom. I do believe that when Jesus returns on the Last Day his arrival will be sudden, he will raise all the dead and separate believers from unbelievers. He will then send the unbelievers to hell and his believing children he will take with him to heaven. For those who are familiar with the terminology, I'm an "a-millennialist." No matter what happens in the weeks and years ahead, the Christian can find his comfort in the Lord's promise through his apostle: "We know that in all things God works for the good of those who love him," Romans 8:28.

Chapter 1 – The Need for This Book

One of the memories I have growing up is that my father subscribed to several newsletters and magazines. That was back in the days before home computers, cellphones and the Internet. I remember titles in our mailbox such as the reputable *Kiplinger Washington Letter*, the extreme right-wing *Spotlight* newspaper, and the *Ruff Times*.

The *Ruff Times* was published from the 1970's until the early 2010's by a Mormon financial advisor and economic prognosticator, Howard Ruff. Mr. Ruff had forecasted a major world economic collapse. In order to prepare for the financial bottom to fall out, Ruff advised his readers to accumulate gold and silver coins and to store food and other necessary supplies in their homes. Howard Ruff's recommendations for food storage came from his Mormon beliefs. He reinforced the ideas from his newsletter in two books, Famines and Survival in America (1974) and How to Prosper during the Coming Bad Years (1978).

Based on the recommendations he read in the *Ruff Times* and other books and periodicals, I remember my dad had canvas bags of junk silver quarters hid in our attic and shelves of extra groceries in our basement. Junk silver is simply any silver coin that has no numismatic value, but its value is simply in the silver bullion the coin contains. The economic disaster Howard Ruff was predicting, however, never arrived. My dad eventually sold his junk silver and our family used up the stored groceries.

Since the 1970's, the United States has witnessed inflation that took the interest rates on car and homes loans, as well as on bank certificates of deposit, to the high teens. We have seen a number of recessions. But the biggest economic drop in most of our lives was the Great

Recession that started at the end of 2008. Many of you may have lost your jobs during the Great Recession. What is even more possible is that you're weekly earnings decreased. Some folks lost their houses because they couldn't make their mortgage payments. Others lost large portions of their retirement savings because they were tied up in stocks, ETF's and mutual funds which declined in value. Retirees have had little if any income from their bank accounts, CD's and investments because the Federal Reserve has kept interest rates low.

During the Great Recession I was living in a major metropolitan area, serving a church with a sizable membership and which also operated a Christian school. Yes, I'm a pastor. We had two pastors, an administrative assistant for both the church and school, five full-time grade school and preschool teachers, and a number of part-time teacher aides. Three years before the Great Recession, we completed a major $2.8 million building program. We had expanded the school and remodeled the church and facility offices. At the time of our building program, local banks would not offer us a loan with a reasonable interest rate, so we went to our national church body for financing. Our monthly mortgage payments were substantial, but we felt that if everyone gave the weekly offerings they promised and if the school grew with tuition-paying students, we would come out just fine.

But then the Great Recession hit. I noticed there weren't as many cars on the freeways going to work in the morning or coming home in the evening. The number of freight trains that passed through our city were fewer and farther between. A number of our church members and school parents lost their jobs. Offerings declined. Our school didn't grow as quickly as we were planning.

Before we knew it, our church and school were almost $100,000 in the red, and we realized that we couldn't continue hemorrhaging money at that rate. We talked seriously about closing our school and releasing staff. My associate pastor accepted a different position in another community and he was not replaced at the time. Instead of layoffs, the entire staff took a substantial pay cut. We also took a step of faith and added a full-time three-year old preschool, which brought in additional funds from school tuition. Our national church body also restructured our mortgage, so our monthly payments were not as large as they had been. We put our confidence in the Lord who told us in the Bible, "Call on me in the day of trouble; I will deliver you, and you will honor me," Psalm 50:15. We also took seriously the apostle Paul's inspired encouragement, "Do not be anxious about anything, but in every situation, by prayer and petition, with thanksgiving, present your requests to God," Philippians 4:6.

Since that time I have moved on to serve God's people in a rural community. Only recently has the value of my former metro home increased to the point where we could sell it. The church I previously served with the large membership and school is doing better.

But what happens the next time there is a recession? We know it will happen. The wisest man who has ever lived, Solomon, wrote in the Old Testament book of Ecclesiastes, "What has been will be again, what has been done will be done again; there is nothing new under the sun," Ecclesiastes 1:9. And what if there is a full-blown depression, like what our parents, grandparents and great-grandparents experienced in the 1930's?

At the time I'm writing this little book there are reputable economists who are forecasting difficult times ahead economically, not just in the United States, but around the world. Radio and TV advertisements try to sell consumers gold coins and bullion because major banks are filling their vaults with gold, preparing for something big. Pension payments to retirees have been being cut. Stock markets around the world look like a roller coaster. Government debt is exploding in size. Many of those who became unemployed during the Great Recession have stopped looking for a job. Folks who made a living wage before the late 2000's are now working at fast-food restaurants and big-box stores for minimum wage. And who knows when the United States will suffer under another major terrorist attack, as we did in 2001?

Are you prepared if our economy, figuratively speaking, suddenly falls off a cliff? Are you ready to provide for and protect your loved ones if terrorists move our government to declare martial law? Can you pick up and leave your home if the local nuclear power plant suffers a meltdown because of an earthquake or storm? What if a rogue nation explodes a nuclear device high in our atmosphere, and our electrical grid and our financial and communication systems stop working for months or even years? Records of our money are kept on electronic servers and storage devices. What if these large super-computers would stop working and there would be no way to access our financial savings and investments? Could you survive?

God never promised us a heaven on earth. In fact, the Bible tells us that life in this world full of sin, evil and trouble will never be easy. "Mortals, born of woman, are of few days and full of trouble," Job 14:1. But for the child of God who believes in Jesus, we're told that the Lord works everything out for our eternal good, Romans 8:28. Paul also wrote to the Romans, "I consider that our present sufferings are not worth comparing with the glory that will be revealed in us," Romans 8:18. God has promised in his Word to answer the prayers of his believing children and that he will always take care of us. King David offered this observation, "I was young and now I am old, yet I have never seen the righteous forsaken or their children begging bread," Psalm 37:25. And then we have Jesus' words from his Sermon on the Mount. They are worth repeating at length:

> "Therefore I tell you, do not worry about your life, what you will eat or drink; or about your body, what you will wear. Is not life more than food, and the body more than clothes? Look at the birds of the air; they do not sow or reap or store away in barns, and yet your heavenly Father feeds them. Are you not much more valuable than they? Can any one of you by worrying add a single hour to your life? And why do you worry about clothes? See how the flowers of the field grow. They do not labor or spin. Yet I tell you that not even Solomon in all his splendor was dressed like one of these. If that is how God clothes the grass of the field, which is here today and tomorrow is thrown into the fire, will he not much more clothe you—you of little faith? So do not worry, saying, 'What shall we eat?' or 'What shall we drink?' or 'What shall we wear?' For the pagans run after all these things, and your heavenly Father knows that you need them. But seek first his kingdom and his righteousness, and all these things will be given to you as well. Therefore do not worry about tomorrow, for tomorrow will worry about itself. Each day has enough trouble of its own," Matthew 6:25-34.

We can depend on our heavenly Father's divine providence. But often, God provides for us, our families and our loved ones through our own actions or the efforts of others. I'm reminded of this story I've heard several times, and maybe you have, too—

A religious man was once caught in rising floodwaters. He climbed to the roof of his house and trusted God to rescue him. A neighbor came by in a canoe and said, "The waters will soon be above your house. Hop in and we'll paddle to safety." "No thanks" replied the religious man. "I've prayed to God and I'm sure he will save me." A short time later the police came by in a boat. "The waters will soon be above your house. Hop in and we'll take you to safety." "No thanks" replied the religious man. "I've prayed to God and I'm sure he will save me." A little time later a Coast Guard helicopter hovered overhead, let down a rope ladder and said. "The waters will soon be above your house. Climb the ladder and we'll fly you to safety." "No thanks" replied the religious man. "I've prayed to God and I'm sure he will save me." All this time the floodwaters continued to rise, until soon they reached above the roof and the religious man drowned. When he arrived at heaven he demanded an audience with God. Ushered into God's throne room he said, "Lord, why am I here in heaven? I prayed for you to save me, I trusted you to save me from that flood." "Yes, you did my child" replied the Lord. "And I sent you a canoe, a boat and a helicopter. But you never got in." [Adapted from "I Sent You a Rowboat," author unknown, from StoriesforPreaching.com]

Paul stressed the importance of taking care of our loved ones when he wrote to his former student, the young pastor, Timothy: "Anyone who does not provide for their relatives, and especially for their own household, has denied the faith and is worse than an unbeliever," 1 Timothy 5:8. I'm also reminded of the inspired words from Proverbs where the author wrote of the wife of noble character. Here is a picture of a godly woman who actively asserts herself to help provide for her family. She is presented as someone we should emulate:

> A wife of noble character who can find? She is worth far more than rubies. Her husband has full confidence in her and lacks nothing of value. She brings him good, not harm, all the days of her life. She selects wool and flax and works with eager hands. She is like the merchant ships, bringing her food from afar. She gets up while it is still night; she provides food for her family and portions for her female servants. She considers a field and buys it; out of her earnings she plants a vineyard. She sets about her work vigorously; her arms are strong for her tasks. She sees that her trading is profitable, and her lamp does not go out at night. In her hand she holds the distaff and grasps the spindle with her fingers. She opens her arms to the poor and extends her hands to the needy. When it snows, she has no fear for her household; for all of them are clothed in scarlet. She makes coverings for her bed; she is clothed in fine linen and purple. Her husband is respected at the city gate, where he takes his seat among the elders of the land. She makes linen garments and sells them, and supplies the merchants with sashes. She is clothed with strength and dignity; she can laugh at the days to come. She speaks with wisdom, and faithful instruction is on

her tongue. She watches over the affairs of her household and does not eat the bread of idleness. Her children arise and call her blessed; her husband also, and he praises her: "Many women do noble things, but you surpass them all." Charm is deceptive, and beauty is fleeting; but a woman who fears the LORD is to be praised. Honor her for all that her hands have done, and let her works bring her praise at the city gate, Proverbs 31:10-31.

Our goal in this little book is to share with you tools, suggestions and ideas you can use to help provide for and protect yourself and your loved ones if our societal structures break down and we find that our survival is dependent on our own actions. But we'll also share portions from God's Word, the Bible, where the greatest advice can be found, especially when it comes to a life of peace with our Creator and eternal life in his heavenly home.

Chapter 2 – Water Is Essential for Life

When scientists send spacecraft such as rovers and satellites to other planets in their search for extraterrestrial life, what is the main thing they look for? Water, of course. Water is essential for all forms of life. Depending on a person's age, water makes up anywhere from about 60% to 78% of the human body. The younger the person, the larger proportion of water. In the recent past, there have been problems with water in major U.S. cities such as Flint, Michigan. A new source of water caused the lead in this city's pipes to poison the water that people drank, cooked with and bathed in for months. The sad result is that innumerable children are now burdened with lowered mental abilities for the rest of their lives. We recall recent droughts in California and places like Ethiopia, Darfur and other places in sub-Saharan Africa. Besides the terrible effects of the Great Depression, the United States suffered a terrible drought in the 1930's in what is commonly referred to as the Dust Bowl. In the Biblical record, there are accounts of drought at the time of Jacob and his sons as well as a drought at the time of the prophet Elisha.

Lack of water causes all sorts of problems. Crops can't grow and people starve. Soil becomes dry and erodes. Top soil blows away. Children cannot develop physically as they should. We have all seen photos of malnourished and dehydrated children that tear our hearts out. In many parts of the world a lack of water results in a lack of electricity, since hydroelectric facilities are unable to produce energy. In severe cases of drought, fires cannot be extinguished. Forests and grasslands, not to mention homes and businesses, go up in smoke. A long-term, severe lack of water can even result in wars between nations.

Water also played an important role in Bible times. As Moses related to us the creation of the universe—under the inspiration of the Holy Spirit—we're told, "Now the earth was formless and empty, darkness was over the surface of the deep, and the Spirit of God was hovering over the waters," Genesis 1:2. When Jesus spoke with the Samaritan woman at Jacob's well, he spoke to her about the water of life which he gives and how he is the promised Messiah:

> Now Jesus learned that the Pharisees had heard that he was gaining and baptizing more disciples than John—although in fact it was not Jesus who baptized, but his disciples. So he left Judea and went back once more to Galilee. Now he had to go through Samaria. So he came to a town in Samaria called Sychar, near the plot of ground Jacob had given to his son Joseph. Jacob's well was there, and Jesus, tired as he was from the journey, sat down by the well. It was about noon. When a Samaritan woman came to draw water, Jesus said to her, "Will you give me a drink?" (His disciples had gone into the town to buy food.) The Samaritan woman said to him, "You are a Jew and I am a Samaritan woman. How can you ask me for a drink?" (For Jews do not associate with Samaritans.) Jesus answered her, "If you knew the gift of God and who it is that asks you for a drink, you would have asked him and he would have given you living water." "Sir," the woman said, "you have nothing to draw with and the well is deep. Where can you get this living water? Are you greater than our father Jacob, who gave us the well and drank from it himself, as did also his sons and his livestock?" Jesus answered, "Everyone who drinks this water will be thirsty again, but whoever drinks the water I give them will never thirst. Indeed, the water I give them

will become in them a spring of water welling up to eternal life." The woman said to him, "Sir, give me this water so that I won't get thirsty and have to keep coming here to draw water." He told her, "Go, call your husband and come back." "I have no husband," she replied. Jesus said to her, "You are right when you say you have no husband. The fact is, you have had five husbands, and the man you now have is not your husband. What you have just said is quite true." "Sir," the woman said, "I can see that you are a prophet. Our ancestors worshiped on this mountain, but you Jews claim that the place where we must worship is in Jerusalem." "Woman," Jesus replied, "believe me, a time is coming when you will worship the Father neither on this mountain nor in Jerusalem. You Samaritans worship what you do not know; we worship what we do know, for salvation is from the Jews. Yet a time is coming and has now come when the true worshipers will worship the Father in the Spirit and in truth, for they are the kind of worshipers the Father seeks. God is spirit, and his worshipers must worship in the Spirit and in truth." The woman said, "I know that Messiah" (called Christ) "is coming. When he comes, he will explain everything to us." Then Jesus declared, "I, the one speaking to you—I am he," John 4:1-26.

The apostle John used the picture of water to illustrate the glories of heaven with Jesus (Revelation 21:6 and 22:1-3), and Peter used the picture of water to show how baptism saves us (1 Peter 3:20, 21).

Water is essential for life. So how do you store water, guaranteeing it's available for you and your family if there is a societal breakdown? Remember that if the electricity is out, sewage treatment plants won't work. Well pumps won't be able to operate. Water from municipal water towers will be available for a while, but that will eventually run out, too. You need water to drink, cook, bathe and clean. What will you do?

The government recommends one gallon of water per person per day and that you should have a minimum supply to last for three days. Some preppers recommend that you should keep a six month supply of water on hand in your home, using five to six gallon water jugs that can be purchased at big-box stores or online. Be sure to use plastic containers that are labeled with the number 2, 4, or 5 recycling symbols. These are considered the safest. Do not use number 3, 6 or 7.

If you store a large amount of water, you can keep it safe for human consumption by adding 8 drops of regular bleach per gallon. If the water becomes cloudy, you can double the amount of bleach to 16 drops per gallon. You can also strain the cloudy water through coffee filters. It's a good idea to boil your water for one minute before you drink it or use it for cooking, especially if it's been stored for a while. If you live over 6500 feet above sea level, you'll want to boil the water for three minutes.

After you read this, it's not necessary to run out right away and buy a dozen six-gallon water jugs—unless, of course, there appears to be an imminent breakdown of American society. What I would suggest, however, is that you start buying gallon jugs of water every time you go to the grocery store. Build up a supply in a dark, cool place in your home. Feel free to use this water for regular daily consumption purposes. Use the jugs in the front of your storage supply, and when you buy new jugs at the grocery store, you can place those in the very back of your supply.

This way, you keep rotating your stock—if you keep the store gallon jugs sealed you shouldn't have to treat the water unless for some reason it's cloudy when you open it. If you keep the water beyond the shelf-life date on the jug, you should boil it before you use it.

One of the things you'll learn in this book is that you don't have to invest a lot of money in your food and water storage. We suggest that you buy extra water and food every time you go grocery shopping. You can store your extra supplies on shelves in your basement or in a pantry close to your kitchen. It's not necessary to purchase those expensive freeze-dried meals and dehydrated food packages that you hear advertised on talk radio or see in magazines, except possibly for your "bug-out" bag, which we'll talk about later.

Think about your parents, grandparents and great-grandparents. Often, many of them would can vegetables from their gardens or keep extra cans of corn and green beans as well as bags of flour and sugar in their pantries and cupboards. They often went for days or even weeks without having to make a trip to the grocery store. You can learn from the wisdom of your ancestors; you don't need to break the bank either, but you can build up your stockpile of food and water over a period of time.

One item you should always keep on hand is a straw water purifier. They aren't that expensive, and they can be lifesavers, especially if you have to leave home and you don't have the ability to take a water supply with you. It probably wouldn't hurt to have a few.

Also, if you know ahead of time that there's going to be a storm or an earthquake or civil unrest, you can fill your bathtub with water. You can also use the water that's in your toilets' storage tanks. Don't drink the water out of the stool and don't drink the water in the toilet tank if it contains bowl cleaners. The reasons should be obvious.

Chapter 3 – Heat, Light and Communications

Back in the late 1990's, my wife and I were close to a family that lived in a rural old house in southern Minnesota. They were members of the church I served. The community they lived in only consisted of a few old houses. There was no store, no gas station, no nothing. They didn't even have a furnace in their house. The house had no insulation. In the winter, they would put quilts and blankets over their windows. They wore long underwear under their regular clothes and never took off their winter coats. When it got real cold they would splurge and turn on electric space heaters. Remember, this was in Minnesota where temperatures in the winter can easily get down to 20 degrees below zero—and that's not even counting the wind chill!

I recall driving home from their place after a visit in the winter, and I thought of the settlers who populated that prairie a hundred and fifty years ago. How could they survive in their sod-houses and log cabins? When it gets real cold here in the North Star State I often wonder about the Native Americans who made this their home long before the settlers ever moved in. How many Sioux and Ojibwa died every winter because of the severe cold? What did my ancestors from Europe think when they arrived and suffered through their first winter on their homesteads? I'm sure my Norwegian ancestors did just fine in the cold, since they had to deal with it in the Old Country, but my German ancestors must have had a rude awakening. I wonder how often they thought to themselves in the middle of January, "What have I gotten myself into?"

My own family got a taste of living the rustic life in 1993 when we lived in a small town in the mountains of North Carolina. We suffered through a major snow storm that brought 18 inches of snow. Life basically stopped because the community only had a couple snow plows and the local folks didn't really know what it was like to drive on snow and ice. What a mess! Unfortunately, the snow also brought down all kinds of tree branches, and the tree branches brought down all sorts of electrical power lines. We were out of electricity for several days.

Fortunately, we had a real fireplace. Our neighbor across the road had an old wood picket fence she wanted to get rid of, so she let us take boards from her fence to burn in our fireplace. The old wood fence boards made great fire wood. We had a nice fire that kept us warm and allowed us to eat warm meals—mostly pork n' beans and hotdogs—but hey, who's complaining? We were very thankful after the electricity came back on and our oil furnace could keep us warm again and we could use our refrigerator and stove.

But how long could we have lived like that? How long could you live like that if there was a national emergency of some sort and electrical power was out for days, weeks or even months? How would you cook your food? How would you store your groceries? How would you light your house after the sun went down?

In the 1970's, there were those with foresight who recognized there may come a time when we might not have electrical power coming into our homes from utility companies. There were a number of organizations and companies that were promoting home wind generation systems. Windmills could be seen over farms, ranches and homes throughout the United States. This technology has now developed to the point where electric utility companies utilize very large wind generators that can be seen for miles. Unfortunately, with local zoning restrictions in many communities, it can be difficult—if not impossible—for homeowners to install their own wind electric generators.

Where wind generators are not allowed, however, more and more folks are installing solar panels. In fact, I drove by a large dairy farm last week that had a couple acres of solar panels. I would imagine they use the electricity generated from the panels to supplement or even to entirely replace the electricity they must purchase to maintain their dairy operation.

In my little part of the world a lot of folks are also making use of their local natural resources by using outdoor wood burners that heat water and pump it into their homes for their hot water radiators. Yes, it can cause a lot of smoke in the air. Yes, it can be stinky and smelly, especially when the people who own those outdoor wood burners use them to burn their garbage, plastic milk jugs, and other items that should be recycled instead. You can certainly buy split wood from various suppliers in the area, but most people go out in the woods and cut up dead, dry trees and haul the wood home in their trucks and trailers.

All of this reminds me of what God told Adam and Eve in the Garden of Eden after he created the universe and our first parents. Yes, I believe in a literal six day creation as it's recorded for us in the first book of the Bible, the Old Testament book of Genesis. After God had finished his creation, he told Adam and Eve, "Then God blessed them, and God said to them, 'Be fruitful and multiply; fill the earth and subdue it; have dominion over the fish of the sea, over the birds of the air, and over every living thing that moves on the earth,'" Genesis 1:28.

God has given human beings everything around us for our benefit. He intends that we use nature ("subdue it") to support us in our earthly lives. This includes using trees, minerals and other natural resources, light from the sun, even the creatures that live in water, on land and in the air, for our survival. Jesus himself made a campfire and broiled fish after his resurrection (John 21:9).

But God also wants us to treat his creation with care and respect. Before Adam fell into sin, we're told, "The Lord God took the man and put him in the Garden of Eden to work it and take care of it," Genesis 2:15. Solomon also wrote, "The righteous care for the needs of their animals," Proverbs 12:10.

But most people in the United States don't live on the farm anymore or even in a rural area. How do you provide your family with electrical power in an emergency if you live in a city or the suburbs? You can purchase electric generators for under $200, and the price goes up from there. Gasoline, propane, or diesel small engines are attached to an electrical generator that provides electricity for your home and appliances. Make sure that you use these generators in a well ventilated area. Carbon monoxide is deadly!

An important use of an electric generator is to maintain your refrigerator and freezer. If you live in a northern climate, however, a generator may not be necessary for food preservation. If it's cold enough outdoors, an unheated garage or shed make a perfect refrigerator or freezer.

One word of warning, however. If there's a major economic or societal crisis and the power is out for weeks or longer, don't let others see you have electric power. Run your generator during daylight hours when the noise it produces can be somewhat masked by everyday neighborhood activities. If everyone else's lights are out in your neighborhood, don't rub it in your neighbors' faces by burning your lights after it gets dark outside. People will definitely notice and in desperate situations they will try to steal or rob you of your generator. This is where being armed can make the difference in surviving a catastrophe.

What are some other things you can have on hand in case you're unable to use your kitchen appliances? Many of us have propane or charcoal grills that we use in the summertime. It would be wise to store a few extra bottles of propane or bags of charcoal and lighter fluid in a cool, dry place. Be sure to keep the propane bottles out of your house! You should also keep on hand boxes of matches and fire starters. If the charcoal or propane run out, you can use the fire starters to help burn wood. Please don't use your grill in your house, unless you want to burn it down or fill it with carbon monoxide!

And what about light? If you can't afford a generator or you don't want to risk conflicts with the neighbors when you have one and they don't, you may want to limit your light use to flashlights and lanterns.

My wife also has an old fashioned oil lamp she inherited from her grandmother. It still has a glass chimney and a fabric wick. She can use candle fluid that is often used for reusable home or church candles. If you're a camper, you might have a camping lantern or two in your garage. Make sure you have plenty of fluid or propane on hand, as well as extra wicks. Be careful with these oil and gas lamps, especially if you use them in your home. They could be a source of carbon monoxide; they could also set your house on fire if you would tip one over while it was lit (especially the old time oil lamps).

But don't forget about having flashlights, battery-operated lights and a healthy supply of glow sticks. There are also flashlights that use a hand-operated crank to generate the power to keep them lit. It's always a good idea to have a supply of flashlights and battery operated lamps on hand, along with a generous supply of rechargeable batteries.

Now you're probably wondering: why would I recommend rechargeable batteries if the power is out? How can a person recharge the batteries if the electrical outlets in your house don't work? Voila! There are such things as solar battery chargers! You can purchase them online for as little as $50.00.

While we're at it, when there's no electricity, there's no e-mail, no telephone, no cable or satellite TV. So how do you communicate? How do you get that important message to your family or friends across town, in a neighboring state or across the country? How do you get your news?

I would imagine that if there was a societal breakdown, a knockout punch on our electrical systems, or some other natural or man-made catastrophe, the government would try to get mail service up and running as soon as possible. So be sure to keep stamps, envelopes and writing paper available. It may have been years since you wrote a letter, but there may come a time when your life or the life of a loved one depends on it.

Other communication tools you might want to keep on hand would be a set or two of high quality walkie-talkies, an emergency radio like you can purchase from the Red Cross, and a citizens-band (CB) radio like truckers use. You may also want to keep your electronic devices in a Faraday cage, which is simply a bag, box or even closet that consists of conductive material (such as tin foil) that would prevent electrical impulses from destroying your electronics. A Faraday cage will protect your electronic equipment in case a rogue nation or group would explode an EMP bomb above us. If you're interested in making a Faraday cage for yourself and your family, just type "faraday" into your web browser. You'll find more than enough information to make it yourself.

Chapter 4 – Wild Game, Fish and Protection

If a national emergency extends beyond days, weeks or even months, you very well may run out of food. If your home food supply becomes depleted or stolen by the less fortunate in your community, or if you have to leave your home for safer surroundings, you may need to hunt and fish for your daily meals.

In some parts of the country, folks are used to hunting and fishing and eating what they have caught, trapped or hunted. Others may be averse to consuming the blessings of God's creation. This can be especially true for those who have lived in cities and suburbs all their lives. People who have lived in small towns or rural areas are more aware of how our food supplies come from farms and feedlots. But what are you going to do if there's no truck transportation to deliver food supplies to your local grocery store? What if the electricity isn't turned back on for a very long time, and grocery store coolers, refrigerators and cash registers can't operate?

As believers in Jesus, we trust our Savior will always keep us in his care. We know the Lord will provide. We have some wonderful promises of God's providence in the Bible:

Psalm 50:15, "Call on me in the day of trouble; I will deliver you, and you will honor me."

Psalm 37:25, "I was young and now I am old, yet I have never seen the righteous forsaken or their children begging bread."

Romans 8:28, "We know that in all things God works for the good of those who love him, who have been called according to his purpose."

God provides for his children, or he uses our needs to bless us in a much greater spiritual or eternal way. Most often he uses natural means to take care of us—think back to the story we shared in the first chapter about the man on his roof at the time of a major flood. Sometimes the Lord provides for us miraculously, like he did when he fed the 5,000 men near the Sea of Galilee during his earthly public ministry, with just five loaves of bread and two small fish (John 6:1-15). The number 5,000 did not include the women and children, so there were actually many more than 5,000!

So how can God use us to provide for our families and loved ones in times of extreme need?

If you live in an area where streams, rivers and lakes are plentiful, it's always a good idea to have the tools to catch fish. For survival purposes, you don't need bulky fishing tackle boxes or expensive rods and reels. What you do need, however, is fishing line, hooks and weights. You can always tie the line to a long stick. You can always dig up worms for bait or find bugs or other things fish like to eat. It would also be wise to have a valid fishing license from your state. If the social structure breaks down and law enforcement is on edge and looking for any excuse to detain people, you don't want to be caught fishing (or hunting for that matter) without a proper license.

I haven't done it for several years, but when I was in elementary school I was taught how to use traps to capture animals. It's like riding a bike—when you learn how to trap, you never forget. You can purchase snare traps and spring traps on the Internet. Spring traps are available for about $8.00 and up. There are also dog-proof traps available, especially if you're concerned about mistakenly capturing pets. There are also live traps that don't harm the animals you catch. Probably the most favorite brand of live trap that's been around for years is Havahart.

A word of warning when handling wild animal carcasses—it's important to wear gloves so the mites and other small pests from their fur and skin don't infect you. At his lake house, my dad and his neighbor were having problems with raccoons getting into the garbage cans at night. They trapped the raccoons and disposed of the carcasses. But they never used gloves. A short time later, my father was diagnosed with encephalitis and was very ill in the hospital for several weeks. Not too long after that he was diagnosed with Parkinson's disease. Did the mites from the raccoons contribute to his illnesses? I couldn't prove that for sure, but I later heard a news report on the radio that mites from raccoon fur could cause human neurological illnesses. So be careful and wear gloves!

Some might find this chapter disgusting as we talk about killing and eating wild animals. I recognize there are many who feel we should treat all of God's creation with respect. That is certainly a part of good Christian stewardship. God has given us all of creation to care for, just as Adam tended the Garden of Eden before the fall into sin (Genesis 2:15). But God also gave us the blessings of nature for our sustenance. After they were cast out of Eden, Adam and Eve were allowed to eat the plants of the field (Genesis 3:18). It was not until Noah and his family left the ark after the flood, however, that human beings were allowed to eat the meat of animals. This is what God told Noah: "Everything that lives and moves about will be food for you. Just as I gave you the green plants, I now give you everything," Genesis 9:3. While they travelled for forty years in the Sinai, God sent the Israelites quail in the evening to eat for food. In the morning, he made manna appear on the ground like dew which the people baked

(Exodus 16 and Numbers 11). A number of Jesus' disciples were fishermen. Even Jesus ate fish (Luke 24:42). But let's make sure we use the gifts God has given us in nature with respect, since the Holy Spirit through the apostle Paul informs us that even nature longs for Christ's second coming and the future glory of God's children (Romans 8:18-23).

When you need to provide for yourself from nature or when you need to defend yourself, one tool that no one should be without is a good knife. The only one I recommend is the K-Bar that has been used for generations by the United States Marine Corps. You can purchase a USMC K-Bar for as little as $65.00 online. Maybe you're a veteran and have one already.

In any survival situation where you would need to protect yourself or provide food, it's important to have firearms available. I've used and handled firearms since I was in middle school. I still remember the firearms safety classes I was required to attend before I could go small game hunting. If you have never handled a firearm before, it's important that you take a safety class for handling both long guns (rifles and shotguns) and handguns. I would strongly encourage you that you take the safety classes before you purchase a firearm, that is, if you don't have one already. Also make sure that you have your firearms safely stored in your house. The last thing you want is a little child getting their hands on one!

In the past few years, millions of Americans have obtained their conceal carry permits. This allows an ordinary citizen to carry a concealed firearm on their person for personal protection. In most, if not all states, a safety class is required before you can obtain a permit to carry a firearm in this way. It's also important to obtain conceal carry insurance, just in case you ever would have to use your weapon. For more information you can check out the website of the U.S. Concealed Carry Association at www.usconcealedcarry.net.

I would also suggest that before you purchase a firearm, especially a handgun, you should visit a gun shop and try the "feel" of the firearm in your hand. Is it comfortable? Would it be easy to use? Would it be sufficient for what you need it for? Some gun shops may even allow you to try out the firearm in their gun range.

I have a small Beretta semiautomatic that I inherited, which is easy to conceal. But there are all sorts of well-made firearms that may fill your needs better. Some of the brands available other than Beretta are Smith & Wesson, Glock, Sig Sauer, Springfield, Sturm Ruger, Colt, Walther, Browning and Luger.

It's also important that you have a rifle or a shotgun. Some folks have both. I know families who have a number of rifles and shotguns. A popular rifle that has received a lot of publicity the past few years is the AR-15. In the hands of the mentally and emotionally disturbed, such a weapon can cause a great deal of damage and heartache. I, for one, am a gun owner who unapologetically believes there should be some sort of psychological background checks for people who want to purchase a firearm. But an AR-15 is also a vital and necessary tool for obtaining food or for self-defense in desperate situations. If you don't have a rifle yet, be sure to check out some outdoor magazines and see what's being advertised. Also, don't hesitate to visit a gun shop and see what the professionals would suggest for your personal needs.

My first firearm was a bolt-action Mossberg 20-gauge shotgun. I now have a Mossberg 12-gauge pump shotgun. I have a barrel for using bird-shot for ducks, pheasants and small game. I also have an interchangeable barrel for using slugs when I go deer hunting. For personal protection I would recommend using slugs or buckshot in your shotgun. Again, be sure to visit a gun shop and see what they would recommend for you.

It may be unsettling for some of our readers to digest all this about knives and firearms. Let me try to alleviate your concerns by considering one of the most beautiful and comforting portions of the Bible. King David composed the 23rd Psalm by the inspiration of the Holy Spirit. I'd like to share it with you in the King James Version:

> The Lord is my shepherd; I shall not want.
> He maketh me to lie down in green pastures: he leadeth me beside the still waters.
> He restoreth my soul: he leadeth me in the paths of righteousness for his name's sake.
> Yea, though I walk through the valley of the shadow of death, I will fear no evil: for thou art with me; thy rod and thy staff they comfort me.
> Thou preparest a table before me in the presence of mine enemies: thou anointest my head with oil; my cup runneth over.
> Surely goodness and mercy shall follow me all the days of my life: and I will dwell in the house of the Lord forever.

"Thy rod and thy staff they comfort me." You're probably familiar with the shepherd's staff that can often be seen in artists' renditions of Jesus. One painting by Warner Sallman illustrates our Lord with a shepherd's staff in one hand, holding a little lamb in the other. When things get tough, when problems afflict us, when we're burdened with the troubles of living in a sinful world, picture yourself as that lamb, safe in your Savior's arms! The staff in his other hand has a crook on the end so he can reach out and pull sheep and lambs back into the fold when they stray. What a beautiful picture of our Good Shepherd!

But what was the "rod"? It was a solid wooden stick the shepherd used to fight off wild animals that would attack the flock, like wolves and bears and other predators. You could think of the "rod" of the 23rd Psalm as a modern day billy-club that police officers sometimes use. It was an offensive weapon used by ancient shepherds.

Fast forward a thousand years to the life of Christ. Our Lord told us in John 10:14, 15, "I am the good shepherd; I know my sheep and my sheep know me—just as the Father knows me and I know the Father—and I lay down my life for the sheep." Jesus is telling us that he is the Shepherd David wrote about in the 23rd Psalm! Not only does Jesus, our Good Shepherd, fight off the attacks of Satan in our behalf, but he even laid down his life so we, the sheep, could be spared. What a beautiful picture of the gospel, which tells us that Jesus suffered the punishments of hell on the cross in our place, so we could be spared from hell and be declared "not guilty" of sin in the eyes of God!

Now, if our Good Shepherd would use a "rod" to fight off our enemies—if he would lay down his very life for us and then raise it again on Easter—then we should follow his example to protect ourselves and our loved ones from our enemies who would like to do us harm. Ancient shepherds used "rods"; we have weapons like knives and firearms. Let's not misuse these tools of protection and preservation, but may we use them as they're intended to be used.

Chapter 5 – Getting Out of Town

In the Bible, we have a number of examples of folks "buggin' out" for one reason or another—usually in life and death situations. In Genesis 12 Abram and Sarai (later renamed Abraham and Sarah) had to flee to Egypt because of a severe famine in Canaan.

Several years later Jacob and his family moved to Egypt from Canaan because of another famine. This time, Jacob's son, Joseph, was second in command of all the land of Egypt. If you're unfamiliar with the account of Jacob, Joseph and his family, be sure to get out your Bible and read Genesis chapters 37 through 50. In this section of God's Word we have a wonderful example of God's providence—the Lord kept Jacob's family alive during some very troubling times because from this family the Savior of the world would eventually be born.

After Jesus' birth, when the Magi, or Wise Men, came to worship the baby Jesus, king Herod felt threatened by the newborn King and had all the baby boys under two years old in Bethlehem slaughtered. But Jesus step-father, Joseph, was warned in a dream by one of God's angels to flee to Egypt. There Jesus' family stayed until Herod died. Be sure to read Matthew 2 to learn more about the Magi and the flight to Egypt.

Finally, after Christ's resurrection and ascension, Jesus' prophecy concerning the destruction of Jerusalem (Matthew 24:2) was fulfilled in A.D. 70. The Roman army of Titus surrounded and eventually levelled the city and its temple. Hundreds, if not thousands, of people died. But the Christians fled across the Jordan River to a place called Pella.

We hope it would never happen, but there may come a day when you might have to leave your home and community for the safety of your family. You might have to "get out of Dodge," as they used to say in old Western cowboy movies. I wonder how many people left New York City after the attack on the Twin Towers on September 11, 2001.

Or maybe a nearby nuclear plant has a meltdown and an unintended and dangerous amount of radioactive material is released into the air. I'm old enough to remember the Three Mile Island accident in the United States. I'll never forget the pictures I've seen in the National Geographic magazine of the area around the Chernobyl nuclear plant in Ukraine. Then there was the nuclear meltdown of the Fukushima nuclear plant in Japan in more recent times that was triggered by a Tsunami. My family and I currently live less than twenty miles from a nuclear plant that began operating in 1973. If there was ever a major release of radioactivity, we would have to flee at least fifty miles away from the plant. Such a scenario would require us to leave our home at a moment's notice!

Another situation where you might be required to leave your home is in the case of social and civil disorder. What if there were riots in your neighborhood and the corner convenience store was looted? What would you do if marauding bands of desperate people were going house to house, breaking in to find food and shelter?

Two books I would encourage you to read that describe such desperate situations are William R. Forstchen's One Second After (2009), and Ray Gorham's 77 Days in September (2011). Forstchen's book includes a forward by former Speaker of the House Newt Gingrich. The events in both books take place after an EMP attack on the United

States (Electric Magnetic Pulse caused by a nuclear explosion high in the atmosphere). These books, and others, show in some very vivid ways how a family might have to flee their home in a hurry.

If you're a camper or hiker you may have all the supplies and equipment necessary for a quick exit. When I was in high school, my family lived near Seattle, Washington. Because of the nearby mountains, National Parks and hiking trails, I became very interested in backpacking in the high country of the Cascade and Olympic mountain ranges. I've seen a lot of nature in my lifetime, and I still think the Pacific Northwest is one of the most beautiful areas in the United States. I had a large backpack with an aluminum frame, sleeping bag, cooking utensils and all sorts of other equipment I could use.

But if you're not a hiker or a camper, you'll have to start collecting items piece by piece for "buggin' out." You'll have to assemble for yourself and your family what is called a "bug-out bag." Start with a check list for everything you'll need. Keep the checklist handy, because if you do need to leave your home in a hurry, you won't have time to think clearly and make sure you have everything.

Purchase or gather the items you need first—then buy the backpack. If you have a family, you may have to purchase several for your spouse and children. Make sure the backpacks are the appropriate size for each person. Go to one of the large sporting goods retailers and try them on. Find one that will be able to fit all your equipment and still feels comfortable.

I'm not going to spend a lot of time explaining why you need the following items. As you review this list, I'm sure you'll figure out their importance:

Firearms
Knife
Waterproof matches
Fire stick
Firestarter
Insect repellent
Water bottle
Water straw
Protein bars
Dehydrated meals
Can opener
Metal cooking pots
Eating plate, bowl and utensils
Small stove
Sterno
First aid kit
Compass (old fashioned kind)
Sleeping bag
Tarp
Tent
Ground pad
Wool blanket
Clothing – layers
      Long sleeved shirt
      Zip off pants
      Underwear
      Long underwear – depending on climate
      Wool hiking socks
      Medium weight fleece
      Roll up hat with brim
      Gloves
      Rain poncho

Personal items – Toothpaste, toothbrush, deodorant
Rope, cord
Collapsible shovel
Multi-tool
Sewing kit
Candles
Mini LED headlamp
Flashlight
Extra batteries
Whistle
Map of your area or where you plan to head
Silver coins
Roll quarters
$500 in small bills
Binoculars
Toilet paper
Wipes
Soap
Iodine tablets (in case of nuclear fallout)
Passports, drivers' licenses and important personal papers

For your car you should also have the following items ready to go:

Extra gas or diesel fuel
Car rack or trailer
3 days water for each person
Bicycle
Lantern
Extra batteries
First Aid Kit

Keep your vehicle's gas tank full, or as close to full as possible. You can attach the bikes right before you leave your house.

Chapter 6 – The Most Important

There are a number of things we need to discuss yet before we can finish this little book on the Christian's survival during a time of local or national crisis. As a Christian, you cannot maintain your faith in Christ without God's Word, the Bible. Through the gospel, the Holy Spirit works in our hearts. Paul wrote, "Faith comes from hearing the message, and the message is heard through the word about Christ," Romans 10:17. It's from the Bible we learn about our Savior, Jesus Christ: "From infancy you have known the Holy Scriptures, which are able to make you wise for salvation through faith in Christ Jesus," 2 Timothy 3:15. David sung in the Psalms that the teachings of God's Word "are more precious than gold, than much pure gold; they are sweeter than honey, than honey from the honeycomb," Psalm 19:10. King David also said that God's Word "is a lamp for my feet, a light on my path," Psalm 119:105.

I would suggest that your Bible be a convenient size. You want to be able to carry or store it in your backpack. It should be in a faithful but easy-to-read translation from the original Hebrew of the Old Testament and Greek of the New Testament. Personally, I like the New King James Version (NKJV), New International Version (NIV) or English Standard Version (ESV). If you want a study Bible with lots of informative notes, outlines and background information, the only one I would recommend is The Lutheran Study Bible (2009) from Concordia Publishing House.

I cannot overemphasize the importance of having a Bible with you. If society breaks down to the point where martial law is declared, where basic police, fire and emergency services no longer exist, where crowds of rioters indiscriminately destroy property and take human life, you will need God's Word to sustain you. You may have all the food, water, weapons and equipment you need to protect yourself and your family physically, but nothing can comfort and give hope to the human heart like the precious gospel that tells us Jesus has forgiven our sins and has opened heaven's doors for us where we will spend a wonderful eternity with him. I cannot imagine life in this world without that wonderful and tremendous hope!

You should also have available a variety of open pollinated, non-GMO, untreated and not genetically-engineered garden seeds. Every spring I receive in the mail a dozen or so garden catalogues with all sorts of seeds, plants and garden equipment you can order through the mail or online. If there is a breakdown in our electrical grid that would take months or even years to repair and rebuild, we're only kidding ourselves if we think there will be food and other basic necessities in grocery stores. So how will you eat once your food supplies run out? You very well may need to grow your own garden! If there are no stores open to buy your garden supplies, you better have them on hand or you and your family will probably starve to death. There's also plenty of material on the Internet that will teach you the differences between all the different kinds of seeds available for gardeners.

Other items you should have on hand are plenty of plastic garbage bags. There are a thousand-and-one uses for a garbage bag. You should have the large 55 gallon size as well as the smaller three gallon size (for disposing waste of all sorts, etc.). You should also have some building supplies available, maybe stored in your garage, a shed or even your basement. Your tool box should be filled with basic tools such as wrenches, screwdrivers, pliers, saws, hammers, nails, screws, hand drills, etc. You won't be able to depend on an electrical supply, so be sure you have all manually operated tools. An electric saw will do you no good if there's no electricity! You should also keep on hand several 2 X 4's, plywood sheets and wood planks. You never know when you might have to build something—possibly even a new shelter.

Extra clothing for you and your family should be stored in case of an emergency. This is really important in northern climates where winters get cold. We're talking boots, winter clothes, jackets and parkas. You may also want to keep summer clothes on hand. Without electricity you won't be able to run your central air conditioner or even a window fan. And don't forget extra bedding, towels, washcloths, and anything else you can think of.

There are probably many more things I could have mentioned in this little book about survival for you and your family. But as I mentioned in the introduction, I'm not a "prepper," and I'm not going to go to the extreme and tell you that you need to spend thousands of dollars for preparing for an emergency or a crisis. I have shared with you some common sense ideas that won't break your bank account.

No matter what comes your way, always remember: "I can do all this through him who gives me strength," Philippians 4:13.

Dear reader,

I want to personally thank you for purchasing and reading this little book. I don't pretend this is the last word about making family preparations for potential future disasters, but it gives you a start when it comes to protecting your loved ones and providing for them when "all hell breaks loose." I've read survival books with a Bible verse thrown in here and there, but I believe this is the first such book in which God's Word is integrated with the subject matter of survival in times of a societal breakdown.

I'd like to ask for your honest review on Amazon.com. Whether your remarks would be critical or complementary, I would appreciate your honest feedback!

I'm making my e-mail address available if you'd like to contact me personally. I would be more than happy to answer any questions you might have. You can reach me at Stephen.Kurtzahn@gmail.com.

Finally, I want to share with you my other titles that are currently available on Amazon.com—

Let Your Light Shine! An Evangelism Training Program for Those Who Want to Share the Savior with Others

First Corinthians Bible Study

Meditations on…
    Children and Their Training
    Christian Marriage
    The Last Things
    The Ten Commandments
    The Apostles' Creed
    The Lord's Prayer

Help for Pastors Leaving the Ministry

I hope you'll check out my other books. I appreciate any comments, feedback or questions you may have about anything I've written.

God bless!
Stephen Kurtzahn

About the Author

Stephen Kurtzahn is a Christian pastor who has served large and small churches across the country. He currently serves two rural Lutheran congregations, but he's also worked as a banker and stockbroker. Steve has many interests, especially personal development, time management, finance and economics, emergency preparedness and non-profit development and fundraising. Steve and his wife have been blessed with three children and several grandchildren. He resides in the Upper Midwest.

www.ingramcontent.com/pod-product-compliance
Lightning Source LLC
Chambersburg PA
CBHW072019280526
45788CB00007B/2613